Christmas 1996

For Charlaine —
Love Barbara

The
INSIDE-
OUTSIDE
Book of LIBRARIES

Paintings by Roxie Munro
Text by Julie Cummins

Dutton Children's Books · New York

To my parents, who taught me to love books,
and to my editor, Donna Brooks, who helped
me love to make them   —R.M.

To Blair, my favorite librarian   —J.C.

◆

ACKNOWLEDGMENTS

The author and illustrator gratefully acknowledge the following
people and institutions for their generous help:

Janet E. Baldwin, The Explorers Club; Margueritte Boos,
Ocracoke Library; The California Department of Corrections
and Folsom State Prison; Sally Campbell, Andrew Heiskell
Library for the Blind and Physically Handicapped; Shangyu
Chen, Mid-Manhattan Library of The New York Public
Library; Mike Dakota, Berkeley Public Library Tool Lending
Library; The Denver Public Library Public Relations and
Publications Departments; Debbie Gill and Tish Mulkey,
Plano Independent School District; Library for the Future;
Matt Nojonen, Holmes County Public Library, Millersburg,
Ohio; U.S. Navy Public Relations in Norfolk, Virginia;
Meredith Mundy Wasinger, Dutton Children's Books; Dr.
Terry Webb, Library Director of Kapi'olani Community
College.

On page 6, the jacket images of five books translated into
Chinese were painted by the illustrator in miniature. Thanks
are due to the following publishers for their permission to use
these images:

Jacket image from *The Cat's Quizzer* and *The Cat in the Hat*
used by permission of Random House, Inc. TM and copyright
©1995 by Dr. Seuss Enterprises, L.P.

Jacket image from *Snow White* used by permission of Farrar,
Straus & Giroux, Inc., and Nancy Ekholm Burkert. *Hey, Al*
used by permission of Farrar, Straus & Giroux, Inc., Arthur
Yorinks and Richard Egielski.

Jacket image from *Rumpelstiltskin* by Paul O. Zelinsky used
by permission of Dutton Children's Books, a division of Penguin Books USA Inc. Copyright ©1986 by Paul O. Zelinsky.

◆

Library of Congress Cataloging-in-Publication Data

Munro, Roxie.   The inside-outside book of libraries /
illustrated by Roxie Munro; text by Julie Cummins.   p. cm.
Summary: Illustrations and brief text present all kinds of
libraries, from bookmobiles and home libraries to the
New York Public Library and the Library of Congress.
ISBN 0-525-45608-2 (HC)   1. Libraries—United States—
Pictorial works—Juvenile literature. [1. Libraries.]
I. Cummins, Julie. II. Title.   Z731.M947 1996
027.073—dc20   96-12111   CIP AC

Published in the United States 1996
by Dutton Children's Books,
a division of Penguin Books USA Inc.
375 Hudson Street, New York, New York 10014
Printed in Hong Kong   First Edition
10 9 8 7 6 5 4 3 2 1

CHATHAM SQUARE LIBRARY ◆ Set amidst the busy streets of New York City's Chinatown, this branch library, identified by a blue banner, signifies good things for its community. Chatham Square Library typifies the more than 6,000 neighborhood libraries in the U.S. that reflect their communities' interests and needs. At Chatham Square, books, maps, newspapers, and recordings are available in both English and Chinese. The library also acts as a cultural center, offering programs and meeting space for community groups and special events.

The children's room in the Chatham Square Library is a lively place—like children's rooms in public libraries everywhere. These preschoolers are enjoying story time with the children's librarian, who is using finger puppets to tell rhymes and tales. Throughout the year, activities featuring crafts, videos, music, and of course storytelling serve toddlers to teenagers. Whether reading for school or for pleasure, using the computer, or participating in summer programs, the neighborhood youth (and their parents) know this library has resources, activities, and a helpful staff to serve them.

OCRACOKE LIBRARY ◆ The weathered boardwalk here tells of this library's seaside locale: Ocracoke Island, North Carolina, a 14-mile stretch of land between Pamlico Sound and the Atlantic Ocean. Although the island has only about 650 residents (who must come and go by plane, ferry, or boat), it is not too small to have its own library. The value of a library is measured not by floor space or number of books but by its usefulness to the community it serves.

The intimacy of the one-room Ocra-coke Library is typical of many throughout the United States—small, friendly places where librarians greet their patrons by name and know their reading tastes. Open six hours a week (Fridays 1-4 and Saturdays 10-1), the library is busiest during the summer tourist season. Its collection of 2,000 books covers a range of fiction and non-fiction for children and adults, with a section of large print as well. Of special interest are books on Blackbeard, a pirate who was killed in 1718 in a battle near Ocracoke in the Pamlico Sound.

The LIBRARY of CONGRESS ❖

The splendor of the green-domed roof opposite the Capitol suggests the grandeur beneath it: millions of books and other materials that document our nation's cultural heritage. Created in 1800 to serve Congress, the Library of Congress was originally housed in the Capitol. After the British set that building on fire in 1814, burning all the books, Thomas Jefferson offered to sell his personal library of 6,000 volumes. Congress bought it and erected this impressive Italian Renaissance building bearing his name. As the collection grew, two more buildings were added: the John Adams in 1939 and the James Madison in 1980. The nation's library, the largest in the world, now serves the general public. Its collections continue to grow at the rate of ten new items a minute.

With its ornamental ceiling, stained-glass windows, and statuary, the Rotunda Reading Room forms an awe-inspiring center for the library. A computer catalog and CD-ROM indexes help users find what they are looking for among the 100 million items that the library owns. In addition to books, including children's books from 1870 to the present, it has many specialized collections: manuscripts, maps, photographs, movies, and radio transcripts. The library also administers the U.S. Copyright Office, registering books and other original materials to protect the ownership of their creators. It receives and keeps one copy of every book copyrighted, including this one.

ANDREW HEISKELL LIBRARY *for the* BLIND *and* PHYSICALLY HANDICAPPED ◆ The cane, the dog, and the wheelchair are the first clues that this library is unusual. Part of a national network designated to serve people with visual and other physical impairments, this branch in New York City is equipped with specially formatted materials and machines that enable users to enjoy favorite books and magazines, study, or just browse. Readers who cannot see regular print have many options here: "talking books" on both disk and cassette, books in braille, large-print books, a Kurzweil machine (which converts printed text into the sound of speech), and closed-circuit television magnifiers that enlarge a page of text up to 60 times.

With his fingertips, this young patron is reading a story in braille, a method of writing that uses patterns of raised dots. Its 19th-century French inventor, Louis Braille, was blinded at age 3 and developed the touch system when he was 15. The 63 different dot formations represent letters (including capitals), numbers, and punctuation. Using the index fingers of both hands, readers can average about 125 words per minute. The children's room at this library caters to a sense of touch with puzzles, puppets, and tactile objects like jingle bells, globes, and plastic dinosaurs that help visually impaired children identify shapes. Both children and adults can borrow braille and recorded books, as well as audio-playback equipment, for home enjoyment.

The braille here reads: "hard to realize that the rustle of a falcon's wings . . ." It is from *My Side of the Mountain* by Jean Craighead George (copyright © 1959 by Jean Craighead George).

EXPLORERS CLUB LIBRARY ◆

This six-story townhouse in New York
City serves as the headquarters of
the Explorers Club, an organization
founded in 1905 to encourage scientific exploration and to serve as a meeting place for explorers and scientists.
Membership is worldwide and includes famous explorers both past and
present such as Sir Edmund Hillary,
Admiral Robert E. Peary, and Sally
Ride. The club maintains an unparal-
leled library here—open by appoint-
ment to its members and the public—
of 25,000 books, maps, and objects
dedicated to scientific exploration and
fieldwork. Memorabilia, paintings,
and sculpture document members'
accomplishments and illustrate the
conquest of frontiers.

Maps and charts are vital to every kind of exploration, so the Sir Edmund Hillary Map Room on the sixth floor of the townhouse has collected over 5,000 of them, including early charts and members' hand-drawn sketches of remote regions. All areas and aspects of exploration are covered by the library's collection, which includes books written by members as well as diaries, photographs, and artifacts from legendary exploits: Admiral Peary's sledge, the globe Thor Heyerdahl used in planning his Kon-Tiki expedition, a giant stuffed polar bear from the Chukchi Sea in the Arctic, and an ancestor totem from New Guinea.

ABRAHAM LINCOLN (CVN 72) LIBRARY, U.S. NAVY ◆ The flurry
of activity aboard this nuclear-powered aircraft carrier, one of seven Nimitz-
class carriers, seems incompatible with the quiet atmosphere of a library. But
the 5,500 men and women who eat, sleep, and work here must also be able to

study and enjoy their leisure time. So, in this special world—where every day 18,000 meals are served and 185,000 gallons of fresh water are made—a small but full-fledged library is tucked below the flight deck on the port side.

Books ahoy! In the library aboard the *Abraham Lincoln,* crew members can
browse comfortably and check out books, videos, CDs, cassettes, and even
computer games. Private work centers offer computers for studying, writing,
or other projects. For keeping up with current events, there are newspapers

and magazines. The most popular is *Navy Times,* a weekly publication that reports on military matters, lists promotions and assignments, and carries news and ads as well. The library is next door to the chapel, so the ship's chaplain does double duty as librarian.

FOLSOM STATE PRISON LIBRARY

Located on the site of an old gold mine, California's second-largest prison was opened in 1880 to relieve overcrowding at San Quentin. Inside the 40-acre granite-wall enclosure, a library houses two separate collections of books for the 3,800 men to use. Folsom's educational programs utilizing the library include literacy workshops, English as a second language, and vocational training, all of which give prisoners (three-quarters of whom are high school dropouts) the chance to increase their skills and complete their education. Inmates who work as clerks in the library earn a day off their sentence for each day worked.

Without the more than 500 prison libraries in the U.S., those imprisoned would not have ready access to ideas and information. Federal law requires prisons to provide a law library adequate to assist inmates in the preparation and filing of legal papers. Use of Folsom's 5,000-volume law collection has motivated several men to become paralegals after they were released. In Folsom's recreational library, which contains 20,000 books, Westerns are the most popular reading. The library purchases best-sellers monthly and subscribes to newspapers in five languages. It keeps a section of children's books, too, for fathers to read with their children during visiting hours. The library is open daily from 8 A.M. to 8 P.M.

Tool Lending Library
Tues-Wed 12-7:30
Thurs 1-5:30
Fri-Sat 10-5:30
Sun-Mon CLOSED

Please have library card ready

TOOL LENDING LIBRARY ◆ A wheelbarrow, a ladder, and a cement mixer are unexpected items to see lined up outside a library, but at the Berkeley Public Library Tool Lending Library in California, they're as common as books. Begun in 1979, the TLL has over 2,000 home repair and gardening tools available free of charge to residents ages 18 or older who present their library cards. The tools may be borrowed for up to three days. Each tool has its own bar code for checkout, patrons may place reserves, and the library charges overdue fines ranging from 50¢ to $15.00 a day, with additional fees for damage.

Of the 250 different kinds of tools that can be borrowed, the most popular are Weed Eaters, hedge trimmers, demolition hammers, and electric snakes. From large items like piano dollies and table saws to small tools like drill bits and putty knives, all the equipment is organized and stored according to size and

shape, so the staff can locate each tool easily. The branch library next door adds
the finishing touch by offering a sizable collection of how-to books and videos for
a wide range of do-it-yourself projects.

INTERNET & WORLD WIDE WEB ◆ This maze of circuitry is the inside of a modem, seen close up. A common use of the modem is to link computer users to the Internet, a network of thousands of interconnected computers around the world at places like universities, libraries, businesses, or government

agencies. A popular way to use the Internet is through the World Wide Web,
which allows you to jump from one computer site to another and explore what is
there via a series of graphic directories called "pages." A mere click lets you
read all kinds of text, view pictures, watch animations, or listen to music.

These two students, one at Kapiʻolani Community College in Hawaii, the other at the Denver Public Library, are thousands of miles apart. Yet, via computer, they can tap into the same information. Because the Internet has no geographical boundaries, each can gain access to library catalogs at major universities, read research papers, look at sports-team home pages, or even contact the space shuttle. Sitting in Hawaii, she could view a photo of an old frontier map from the Denver Library collection; he could learn Hawaiian from an audio file offered by the community college. The Internet constitutes a library without walls.

MEADOWS ELEMENTARY SCHOOL LIBRARY ◆ "What's Happening?" asks the sign in the library of Meadows Elementary School in Plano, Texas. The answer is the bustle of activity these fourth graders create as they look up home-work answers, prepare reports, read, and get ready for Children's Book Week.

The 98,000 school library media centers in the U.S. provide all kinds of materials to stimulate students' curiosity and imagination. These children can explore books, videos, science models, computers, and other special items like frontier trunks containing things that convey how Texas settlers lived and worked.

There's a mouse in the school library! But kids use this one to click onto a computer program called the Kid's Catalog. It's a computerized catalog enhanced with pictures and words that help students find books and other materials in their library. Symbols represent categories such as Science, Scary Stuff, or

Famous People. Click, and you see a listing of books the library owns under that
category. Or you can click to search for specific titles or authors. Click again,
and a floor map appears that pinpoints the exact location of a book.
This school library is up and running!

HOME LIBRARIES ◆ On the outside, these buildings are all different. But
inside, they have one thing in common. The families who live here each have a
home library. When people care about things they've read or heard—in books
or magazines, on tapes or CDs—they want to have them on hand to reread and

refer to. So they keep them, and soon they have a library. Depending on how people use them, books may be found in all kinds of nooks, corners, and shelves around the house—the bedroom, kitchen, family room, hall, garage—even the bathroom!

Your own library needn't be fancy or neatly organized. It can be a simple shelf or even a trunk. What matters is that *you* have chosen the books that are there. Some people keep books in their libraries that they haven't yet read—to look forward to reading. Others look fondly upon their libraries for the favorite characters and scenes, authors and ideas they've already enjoyed and will enjoy again. Few things offer the lifelong pleasures that books do. From spellbinding stories to true adventure, from humorous poetry to mathematics and biography, books enable us to laugh, to dream, to hope—and to envision the future.

BOOKMOBILES (opening pages) ✦ The first bookmobile was a single horse-drawn van that in 1905 carried collections of books to people living in rural areas of Maryland. As motor power has replaced horsepower, traveling libraries have grown from simple wagons to air-conditioned vehicles equipped with cellular phones, CD-ROMs, and an average of 3,000 books. Today, over 1,000 bookmobiles make library service available to children and adults in a variety of settings. These mobile units stop at housing projects, shopping malls, schools, and senior citizen homes, as well as outlying, sparsely populated areas. Slanted shelves prevent the books from falling as the bookmobile travels over rough streets or rutted roads.

THE NEW YORK PUBLIC LIBRARY (jacket) ✦ Two marble lions named Patience and Fortitude guard the most recognizable library in the United States—The New York Public Library's famous research building at 42nd Street and Fifth Avenue. Beneath the ornate ceiling of the main reading room, a quarter of an acre in size, 700 people can sit and read. With 82 branches, 4 research centers, and a collection of over 50 million items, the NYPL is the largest library system in the nation, serving over 8 million people annually. The majestic central building symbolizes all public libraries, where everyone—rich or poor, young or old—has equal access to the wealth of knowledge that is our heritage. As a treasure-house of thought from which to project the future, as a repository of ideas both familiar and provocative, libraries safeguard intellectual freedom for us all.